Cambridge
The Watercolour Sketchbook

LAURENCE KING

A Talisman Book for Laurence King

First published in 2016 by

Talisman Publishing Pte Ltd
talisman@apdsing.com
www.talismanpublishing.com

Laurence King Publishing Ltd
361–373 City Road
London EC1V 1LR
United Kingdom
email: enquiries@laurenceking.com
www.laurenceking.com

Paintings © 2016 Graham Byfield
Text © 2016 Marcus Binney
Editor Kim Inglis
Creative Director Norreha Sayuti
Designers Foo Chee Ying, Stephy Chee
Studio Manager Janice Ng
Publisher Ian Pringle

A catalogue record for this book is available
from the British Library

ISBN: 978-1-78067-690-6

Printed in Singapore

Front Cover *Bridge of Sighs.*
Back Cover *King's College.*
Previous Page *Great Gate, Christ's College.*
Right *Master's Lodge, St Catherine's College.*
Far Right *King's College, Clare College and the
          Gibbs Building.*

Cambridge
The Watercolour Sketchbook

Paintings by Graham Byfield
Written by Marcus Binney

Contents

The Trinity College triple-arched bridge over the
Cam was designed and built by James Essex
in 1763-65. It is a simple Classical architectural
work, plain and dignified. Of course, a punt
along the River Cam is a "must" for any visitor:
a number of licensed operators give 45-minute
punt tours which afford tranquil views of the
world-famous Cambridge College Backs.

Early Days

Cambridge is renowned the world over as a university town. Yet it began, like so many towns as a river crossing, first a ford and then a bridge and incidentally the only bridge to give its name to a county rather than a town. The river was no broad or mighty flowing torrent, but the usually placid waters of the Cam, which flows north into the Great Ouse and then to the sea at King's Lynn.

The bridge was built in the 9th century on a vital route serving much of eastern England. All traffic from fertile Essex, London and the south east which was destined for the north east had to cross the river at Cambridge. To the north and east lay the great bog of the East Anglian fens, not drained and made into fertile farmland until the 17th century. When the Normans invaded England in 1066 it was so impenetrable and treacherous that the rebellious Hereward the Wake evaded capture for 20 years in the marshlands around Ely.

English medieval towns prospered thanks to the charters for markets granted them by Norman and Plantagenet kings. Cambridge became the venue for one of the most famous fairs of medieval England, held annually on Stourbridge Common. At its peak it was the largest fair in Europe, the inspiration for John Bunyan's *Vanity Fair*. It was one of four major Cambridge fairs — the others were Garlic Fair, Reach Fair and Midsummer Fair.

The Stourbridge Fair dated from a license granted in 1199 by King John to the Leper Chapel in Cambridge to hold a three-day fair exempt from taxes. The first fair was held in 1211 on the Feast of the Holy Cross on September 14 on the common beside the Cam. Barges brought goods by river; there were roads to London and Newmarket.

"This fair," wrote Daniel Defoe in his Tour through the whole island of Great Britain, "is not only the greatest in the whole nation, but in the world; nor, if I may believe those who have seen them all, is the fair at Leipzig in Saxony, the mart at Frankfort-on-the-Main, or the fairs at Nuremberg, or Augsburg, any way to compare to this fair at Stourbridge."

He described the huge variety of merchandise, with stalls including "goldsmiths, toy-shops, brasiers, turners, milliners, haberdashers, hatters, mercers, drapers, pewterers, china-warehouses, and in a word all trades that can be named in London".

The market place, known as Market Hill, operates every day of the week, as a general market from Monday to Saturday and on Sunday as a local speciality food, arts and crafts market. There has been a market in Cambridge since Saxon times confirmed by the town charter of 1207.

Town and Gown

Senior dons in their official scarlet robes which they wear for special ceremonies.

Thus it was that town came before gown. Cambridge attracted monks and nuns who set up numerous houses here from the 12th century onwards. The four great orders of friars — Dominicans, Franciscans, Carmelites and Augustinians — had important establishments in Cambridge, which were to play a leading role in the early years of the university. The nearby Augustinian Priory at Barnwell dates from 1112, the Benedictine Nunnery of St Rhadegund from 1133, St John's Hospital (an Augustinian House) from 1135. The Franciscan House appeared soon after 1224, the Carmelites in 1249, the Friars of the Order of Bethlehem in 1257, and the Friars of the Penitence in 1258.

Why did England's two greatest university towns emerge in remote rural areas, a considerable distance from great medieval cities such as London, Winchester and York? The answer, in a word, was wool. Oxford was the gateway to the Cotswolds which produced the finest fleeces in Europe, many bred on great monastic and abbey estates. So it was with Cambridge, home to the great abbey of Ely, mentioned in the Domesday book as having 13,400 sheep on its lands. In the Fens there were four other major monastic houses as well as Ely Cathedral Priory, namely Thorney Abbey, Croyland Abbey, Ramsey Abbey and Peterborough Abbey.

Beyond was the rich sheep farming country of Norfolk. When kings like Richard I were taken prisoner, the ransom was paid in wool. The Lord Chancellor himself sat on a woolsack in Parliament. The Barons in 1297 stated the wool of England amounted to half the value of the land.

Sheep produced the great wool churches of Oxfordshire and Norfolk and fed the growth of the two universities. Later, in the Middle Ages, monastic estates were repeatedly diverted to endow new and expanding colleges. Even today East Anglia has the greatest wealth of medieval buildings in Britain. They have survived largely because, when England

Sheep gently grazing on Sheep's Green, with the city beyond.

turned Protestant at the Reformation, the lucrative markets of Flanders were closed, and centuries of unequalled prosperity came to an end. Poverty is a great preserver.

The first universities as we now know them were in great cities, notably Paris and Bologna. In Paris, the university grew around the cathedral from the beginning of the 12th century. In Bologna, the university was based on canon and civil law and medicine. Oxford also began later in the 12th century when famous teachers began to lecture there, boosted by an Order of Henry II in 1167 that all students in France should return to England. In 1209, a serious riot took place in Oxford between town and gown, prompting an exodus of scholars to Cambridge. The birth of Cambridge came as new universities were established in the leading Italian cities of Padua (1222), Pisa (1343) and Pavia (1361).

By 1231, there was a considerable community of students at Cambridge; Henry III announced punishment of disorderly scholars by the Sheriff and fixed the rents of lodgings in the town. This reflected the recurring battles between town and gown in the Middle Ages. In Cambridge, as at Oxford, there were frequent "strifes, fights, spoilings, breaking open of houses, woundings and murder betwixt the burgesses and the scholars".

The Medieval undergraduate entered the university aged about 14 and lived in lodgings or in a hostel under a master. He took a threefold course of Latin grammar, logic and rhetoric. At the end he was put to a test by disputation and became a Bachelor of Arts. He then proceeded to a fourfold course of arithmetic, geometry, music and astronomy, becoming a Master of Arts and qualified teacher.

Clare Bridge's magnificent wrought iron gates allowing you to enter the college across the Cam.

In 1284, Peterhouse was founded by Hugh de Balsham, the Bishop of Ely. Clare College was founded in 1326 by Elizabeth de Burg, Countess of Clare, the first of many colleges to be founded and endowed by women. Pembroke College was founded in 1347 by Mary de St Pol (widow of the Earl of Pembroke). Gonville Hall was founded in 1384 by Edmund Gonville, a Norfolk rector. Trinity Hall followed in 1350, founded by William Bateman, Bishop of Norwich. By contrast, Corpus Christi College was founded in 1352 by two town guilds.

The greatest college foundation of the 15th century was King's College, instituted in 1441 by Henry VI as a sister college to Eton. King's was not open to scholars from other schools until the middle of the 19th century. Queens' College was founded in 1448 by Margaret of Anjou, wife of Henry VI, known for her splendid household. Noted as "a most handsome woman" by the Milanese ambassador, she was keen on riding and hunting. In her petition to the king requesting permission for the foundation she refers to her desire to emulate Elizabeth de Clare and Mary de St Pol.

The oldest post box in Cambridgeshire by King's College.

On the accession of Edward IV, his Queen, Elizabeth Woodville, who he had married in secret, became co-foundress. St Catharine's College was founded in 1473 by a provost of King's and Jesus College in 1496 by the Bishop of Ely on the site of a decayed nunnery.

John Fisher, elected Chancellor in 1504, was the first holder of a Professorship of Divinity established by Lady Margaret Beaufort, mother of Henry VII. On his advice she founded Christ's College in 1505 and St John's College in 1511. Fisher was

Henry VIII, the founder of Trinity College in 1546, is remembered by this statue at the gatehouse of the college.

a pioneer of renaissance scholarship in Cambridge, bringing Erasmus to Queen's in 1510 to become the first teacher of Greek at Cambridge.

Fisher was probably responsible for setting up the first printing press in the University. John Siberch, a friend of Erasmus, printed the first Cambridge book in 1521. Thirteen years later, in 1534, Henry VIII granted a charter to the university authorising the appointment of printers to produce "all manner of books". Today, Cambridge University Press ranks as the world's oldest publishing house as well as the second largest university press in the world (after Oxford).

The Tudors played a key role in expanding teaching from Divinity to secular subjects. The Dissolution of the Monasteries brought the end to the numerous religious houses of Cambridge. Buckingham College, a hostel for Benedictine monks, was re-founded as Magdalene College in 1542. Henry VIII proved a strong supporter of the university, founding Regius Professorships in Divinity, Civil Law, Physic, Hebrew and Greek. In 1546, he merged a group of ancient hostels into Trinity College, a college of "literature, the sciences, philosophy, good arts and sacred theology".

Queen Elizabeth I regarded both Oxford and Cambridge as bulwarks of church and state. Two colleges founded in her reign were Emmanuel College, founded in 1584 on the site of a Dominican house by Sir Walter Mildmay, and Sidney Sussex College, founded in 1596 on the site of a Franciscan house by Frances Sidney, Countess of Sussex.

The 16th century also witnessed the final change from medieval hostels to colleges with resident scholars. Generally, hostels were of small size consisting of one or more houses. They maintained their popularity well after the founding of colleges. Dr Caius, writing in 1573, observed "they were held in good repute by those who devoted themselves to literature, and were crowded with students. Their inmates dined and supped together, as men do who have to lead a common life, and to share a common lot…. Each student lived at his own charges…. Now however they are all deserted, and given back into the hands of the townspeople, apart from a few taken over by Colleges."

Cambridge, so well endowed by the Tudors, remained important politically under the Stuarts. In the Civil War, while Oxford rallied to the King, with the colleges selling all their silver to support his army, Cambridge sided with Parliament and Cromwell. Cromwell was MP for Cambridge and was supported by Cambridge men such as the poet John Milton and the founder of the Royal Society, John Wilkins, a Master of Trinity.

In the later 17th century, Cambridge first became famous for the study of mathematics with the appointment in 1669 of Isaac Newton to the recently founded Professorship of Mathematics. In 1665–7, Newton discovered the laws of motion and gravity, and the calculus. Following the publication of Newton's *Principia* in 1687, Cambridge established a supremacy in mathematical studies which it has never lost.

In the 18th century, Cambridge slumbered less than Oxford, but this was the era when, thanks to the Scottish Enlightenment led by luminaries such as David Hume and Adam Smith, Edinburgh and Glasgow became the chosen universities for those in search of inspired teaching.

In 1807, work began on Downing, the first new college since the 16th century. The university entered a period of gradual reform. This centered on the abolition of religious tests which were only finally removed in 1871. Soon after came the provision that a college fellowship could be held by a married man. New triposes were established in Natural Sciences in 1851, Law in 1859 and History in 1870, extending the range of teaching and study. The foundation of the Cavendish Laboratory in 1871 established the supremacy of Cambridge in experimental Physics. Women students first appeared at Girton College in 1869, followed shortly after by Newnham College. In 1881, women were allowed to take tripos examinations but not to proceed to degrees.

All this led to a large increase of undergraduates from 1,526 in 1862 to 3,676 in 1914. Numbers were reduced greatly during World War I when 2,000 members of the university were killed and 3,000 wounded on active service. In World War II a larger number of undergraduates (mainly students of Medicine, Physics and Engineering) remained. In 1945, as in 1919, large numbers returned from the services and quickly filled the colleges with numbers of undergraduates approaching 7,000. In 1948 women were granted full membership of the university and New Hall opened in 1954 as a new women's college.

A sunny day spent in Cambridge is intoxicating. Here is a town — since 1951 a City — which is the epitome of one of England's greatest contributions to the visual arts, the Picturesque. It has grown round a pattern of ancient roads and lanes with a market place at its centre. The winding layout of its roads and hidden lanes ensures that it is a city that presents constant surprises and delights as you explore. Better, this abiding picturesque quality has been relatively little spoiled by the modern world and its obsession with town planning improvements.

Indeed, if one city had to stand for all that is fine, inventive, lovely and sensitive in English architecture, it is Cambridge. The university town can claim 1,000 years of architectural glories beginning with the visibly Anglo-Saxon tower of St Bene't, continuing with the massive Norman arches of Holy Sepulchre, one of England's five round churches, and the barely altered St Mary Magdalene (also mid 12th century), which began as a hospital chapel to a Leper Colony. Another marvel is the School of Pythagoras dating from 1200 (actually a very early upper floor hall house).

Though colleges grew from monastic foundations, they have much in common with the great noble houses of the later Middle Ages and Tudor period. They share the layout around a court entered through a gatehouse with a great hall open to the roof timbers. Typically, there is a raised dais at one end and a screens passage at the other, shielding view of the entrance to kitchen pantry and buttery. The characteristic Oxbridge staircase arrangement leading to rooms or sets of rooms on each landing is similar to the lodgings found in great 15th-century houses. To these were added college chapels and, from the 15th century, a first-floor library for fellows. Second courts followed and later a third and occasionally a fourth court. The Cambridge gateways are an impressive group, often in the form of towers with medieval doors and often a smaller doorway for those on foot. Those of Trinity and St John's form a splendid pair on Trinity Street.

Downing College was begun in 1807, designed by William Wilkins and is a masterpiece in the Greek Revival style.

Murray Edwards College was formerly New Hall and founded in 1954 and is a women-only constituent college. The college was renamed Murray Edwards after a donation of £30 million by Ros Edwards, an alumna, and her husband. This honoured the donors and the first President, Dame Rosemary Murray.

St. Bene't's Church is the oldest building in Cambridgeshire (1025) and is linked by a covered gallery to Corpus Christi College Old Court which is the earliest court in Cambridge (1377).

In the 16th century both the Renaissance and the Reformation changed the course of college architecture. King's College has a magnificent Renaissance chancel screen and stalls dating from the 1530s beneath its Perpendicular fan vaults, clearly influenced and inspired by North Italian and French examples. The chapel, begun at Trinity in 1555 under Queen Mary who reinstated Catholicism, is still Gothic, but the chapels of the two Puritan colleges established in Elizabeth's reign, Emmanuel and Sidney Sussex, both had a chapel oriented north-south, not pointing east in the traditional manner. Caius College has the most conspicuous examples of Italian Renaissance (or "antyq" as it was often called at the time). One is the Gate of Honour (1573–75) in the form of a triumphal arch surmounted by a *tempietto* and then topped by a dome, inspired by both ancient Roman funerary monuments and more recent Loire chateaux.

The statutes of St John's College in 1555 provide a picture of student life: "Each room to have two beds, one occupied by a fellow, or by two, or one, scholars. Only a doctor or college preacher has a room to himself." Not more than four scholars were to be compelled to occupy the same chamber. Carter, writing of St John's in 1753, notes: "The Master's Lodge hath many good and Grand Apartments, but especially the Long Gallery, which is the longest Room in the University, and which, with the library that opens into it makes a most charming view."

The turn of the century brought the creation of Trinity Great Court with a handsome Italian fountain of 1601–2. The mason who built the contemporary master's lodge and hall at Trinity is Ralph Simons, who also built the second court at St John's. Fuller, the historian, noted a rush of building work in the first quarter of the 17th century: "Now begins the University to be much beautified in Buildings, every college is either casting its skin with the snake, or renewing its bill with eagle, having their courts, or leastwise their fronts and gate-houses repaired and adorned."

The middle decades of the 17th century saw good examples of what is called Mannerist, a less pure, more enriched version of Italian Renaissance, with enrichments from Dutch pattern books and a carefree treatment of classical proportions and detail. Good examples are the east range and gatehouse of Old Court at Clare dating from 1638–40 and the imposing Fellow's Building at Christ's of 1640–43. The Chapel at Peterhouse of 1628–32 is equally *sui generis* mixing Gothic and Classical motifs. From the years after the Restoration of Charles II in 1660 are two delightful examples of homespun classicism — the Pepys Library at Magdalene and Emmanuel Chapel and Cloister by Sir Christopher Wren. The chapel front at Emmanuel makes a fascinating contrast with Wren's almost contemporary chapel at Pembroke which is a monumental temple fronting on to Trumpington Street, so correct in proportions and detailing that it could be by Palladio himself.

The mature style of Wren, and indeed English Baroque, is on show in his monumental library at Trinity College raised over an open arcade in the Italian manner. Several of Wren's early designs survive and attached to the one that was executed is a letter explaining the curious way in which the arches are solid: "I assure you where porches are lowe with flat ceilings is infinitely more graceful than lowe arches…. By this contrivance the windows of the Library rise high and give place for the desks against the walls."

One of the most beautiful of all early 18th-century English buildings is the Senate House built in the 1720s by James Gibbs in sparkling white Portland stone. Gibbs's *Book of Architecture*, illustrating his designs for churches, country houses and civic buildings, made him one of the most influential of all British architects, notably in North America. He had studied in Rome and combined the richness of Italian Baroque with the purity of English Palladianism, reflected here in a design where there is hardly a patch of plain wall to be seen. Unusually, the ends of the building are as handsomely treated as the main front.

Gibbs also designed the monumental Gibbs Building (named after him) at King's, which stands beside King's Chapel on the Backs. In style and form the two could hardly be more different and it is an abiding tribute to Gibbs's genius that this is one of the best loved and most photographed groupings in all English architecture.

Less well known is the name of James Essex who worked at several colleges providing the delightful street front of Emmanuel College and the chapel at Clare. Cambridge has prime works of both the Greek and the Gothic Revival. For Greek, there is William Wilkins's Downing, the first college to be laid out as a campus rather than a series of enclosed courts. Wilkins also designed the lively entrance screen of King's, consisting of gatehouse and cloister, an unsurpassed example of "keeping in keeping" (with King's Chapel). More grandiose, yet equally lively, is Thomas Rickman's masterfully composed New Court at St John's. What is now the Gonville and Caius Library built in 1837–40 is a triumph, built to the designs of the immensely accomplished C R Cockerell in his always inventive and bold Classical manner.

Cambridge is rich in Victorian architecture, beginning with one of the first surviving largish railway stations. Dating from 1845, it was designed by Francis Thompson with an entrance front in the form of a 15-arch loggia, later enclosed.

From the 1860s, the university as well as the colleges began to build in earnest as new subjects were added to the curriculum. A large site became available in Free School Lane after the University Botanic Garden moved to Hills Road in 1846. What became known as the new Museums site was progressively filled with an Italianate Lecture Theatre by Salvin in the 1860s, the Gothic Cavendish Laboratory of the early 1870s by Fawcett, J J Stevenson's Elizabethan Chemical Laboratory from the 1880s, and E S Prior's Edwardian School of Medicine (now Zoology) in an English version of Beaux-Arts. The Victorians made numerous extensions to colleges. Alfred Waterhouse, architect of Manchester's Town Hall and London's Natural History Museum, was much in demand, providing residential ranges at Jesus, Trinity Hall and Caius as well as a new hall and library at Pembroke. G G Scott Junior's New Court at Pembroke (1880–83) is an interesting reworking of 17th-century motifs.

T G Jackson built energetically in the Jacobethan style, providing a series of university buildings from 1899, including the Museum of Archaeology and Anthropology. In the courtyard, well worth seeking out, is an outside staircase with carved bear and bison standing guard at the bottom of the steps as well as an iguanodon in an arch on the street front.

The Gibbs Building next to King's Chapel is named after its architect James Gibbs and has an unusual centrepiece with a large Diocletian (lunette) window set over a giant Roman Doric portico inset with arch.

Classic lights embellish the Paths of Trinity College's Courts.

Lord Foster's Law Library was Controversial when first built, but has now settled into its enviroment with the trees and landscaping.

The interwar years saw Lutyens working at Magdalene College and Herbert Baker at Downing. A fine example of this period is the Clare College Memorial Court of 1923–34 by Giles Gilbert Scott, built of special silver-grey bricks from Ruabon, Portland stone dressings and specially made dark glazed Italian roof tiles. The sash windows, it was noted, were snow white not the more usual ivory.

Another handsome feature are the street lamps designed by the great traditionalist Sir Albert Richardson, recently given protected "listed" status. These are in the form of elegant tapering fluted columns, 21 feet tall, with cylindrical lanterns and are now known as Richardson Candles.

Cambridge is the place to see post-war architecture at its most bold and inventive *and* its most controversial. Sir James Stirling's History Library came close to being pulled down because dons and students thought it dysfunctional. There was even a revolt among readers at noise levels in Lord Foster's sleek new Law Library.

In part, this is the perennial battle between traditional and modern or, to put it another way, between an architecture of our time and an architecture with a sense of place. Cambridge, with its scientific laurels, was a natural place to embrace Modernism and the Modern Movement. The arrival of the Modern, particularly on the Backs, made a powerful impression on me when I was at Cambridge in 1963–66 studying History of Art in the Faculty of Architecture. Here amidst a scene that was still 18th century in feeling was the bright white ziggurat of the Cripps Building to be followed by St Johns.

It was a confrontation taking place in both Oxford and Cambridge. Bill Bryson, in a famous critique of the new Warden's Quarters at Merton Oxford, wrote: "Finely educated minds at Merton had to say to themselves 'you know, we have been putting up handsome buildings since 1264: let's have an ugly one for a change'."

James Lees-Milne, architectural historian and much-loved diarist described Churchill College as "a beastly building, like a enormous public lavatory", while, to the historian David Cannadine, Stirling's History Faculty of 1963–67 was "a monstrosity... part bunker, part factory, part greenhouse, all folly... ugly, strident, unpopular, aggressive, unwelcoming...".

For my first year, I studied Economics and Politics in the campus buildings by Hugh Casson and Neville Condor on Sidgwick Avenue. These were a loose series of quads raised up on Corbusian *pilotis* to open up views and reduce the sense of enclosure. But the underneath of a building, mostly in shadow, is rarely attractive however sleek the concrete and in flat fen country it opened up the whole place to icy winds which traditional enclosed courts help shut out.

A few years' later, returning briefly to teach, I was confronted with the Modernist/primitivist Senior Combination Room at Downing by Howard, Killick, Partridge and Amis which had been praised in a recent article in *Country Life*. Amidst the harmonious stone ranges in Greek Revival style, I thought this was a monstrous jarring intrusion, its plate glass walls and concrete columns mocking the original as passé. Greek Revival architects like Wilkins were always at pains to use exact, and exquisite, Ancient Greek precedents for their Classical detail and here was a broken pediment open at the top, a Baroque feature which no Grecian would have used.

For their next addition, the Downing Fellows turned to Quinlan Terry, a traditionalist well known for elegant classical designs. But, at Downing, he too adopted a playful Baroque style this time attracting censure from the critic Gavin Stamp for having "ostentatiously ignored the neo-classical character of the buildings". Soon after, Terry added a new library this time with a portico of fluted Greek Doric columns.

The Zoology and Metallurgy Building of 1966–71 by Arup Associates was a new evolution of Modernism intended to reflect its scientific purpose in the emphasis on revealed structure. One writer found its "skinny legs and bulky thorax... echo the improbable zoomorphic doodles of Archigram", a practice famous for cartoon drawings of cities consisting on moving parts.

In Oxford, Christ Church has its Meadows and its image of a city of dreaming spires. Cambridge is more a garden city or city of gardens. According to *Cantabrigia Depicta* (1763) at Christ's: "The Fellows Garden is well laid out, and one of the pleasantest in the University: there are both open and close shady walks, beautiful alcoves, a Bowling-green, and an elegant Summer-house: beyond which there is a Cold-Bath, surrounded with a little Wilderness."

The beauty of the Backs is no accident. In 1779, the greatest of all English landscape gardeners, Lancelot "Capability" Brown, presented a plan to the university to create a greensward of grass in the manner of English house parkland. The plan would involve removing avenues, transforming the river into a lake, planting clumps of trees and removing the bridges as well as college boundaries. It was never implemented, but it was part of the transformation of the river banks into a prime example of borrowed landscape whereby one college enjoys not just a view of its own manicured grounds but of its neighbour's too.

In 1772, St John's College had consulted Capability Brown who laid out a wilderness on the college side of Queen's Road along the Backs which survives today. English parkland is typically grazed by deer or stock and the grass of the Backs consists of immaculately mown lawns, always in pristine condition. The same is true of the college courts where grass is rarely worn, thanks to the convention that neither undergraduates nor visitors can walk on the lawns, only Fellows of the College. "If I were called upon to mention the prettiest corner of the world, I should draw a thoughtful sigh and point the way to the gardens of Trinity Hall," wrote the famous American author, Henry James.

College courts are embellished by spring flowers and flowering shrubs and virtually every college has a fine Masters' or Fellows' garden — Emmanuel's with a pond. Several of these gardens have prize examples of specimen trees grown in sheltered conditions to their prime without nearby trees or buildings restricting their growth. A fine example is the great oriental plane tree in the Fellows' Garden at Emmanuel which inspired the poem *El Arbol* by the Spanish poet Luis Cernuda who lived in the college during World War II.

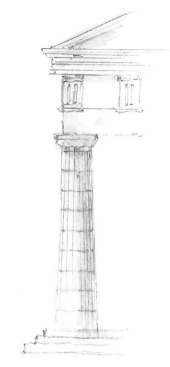

An example of a Greek Doric column, used in the contemporary Downing Library by architect Quinlan Terry.

As everywhere in England, town trees excite passions. The felling of 300-year-old cherry trees in Magdalene College on the bank of the Cam provoked anger among punt operators who had always directed visitors to them in spring.

Visitors throng to see the colleges, but Cambridge is hardly less remarkable for its museums. The Ashmolean in Oxford is the world's oldest university museum, but in Cambridge the Fitzwilliam is its equal. With one of the greatest collections in England, the more splendid because in the Founder's Galleries paintings are not displayed in isolation but surrounded by fine sculpture, furniture and *objets d'art*, it gives the impression of a great nobleman's collection rather than an academic collection.

Its newly cleaned glistening portico eclipses that of the British Museum in sheer richness and pomp. Here, the architect George Basevi moves on from the chaste elegance of the Regency Greek Revival to full Roman Imperial grandeur reflecting the ascendant British Empire. Giant porticoes of eight columns are rare in Britain, and here they are extended by colonnades and pilasters.

The museum was built to house the bequest of the 7th Viscount Fitzwilliam of Merrion who died in 1816 leaving a superb collection of fine books, illuminated manuscripts, autograph music, drawings, engravings and old master paintings including prized works by Titian, Veronese and Palma Vecchio which he bought at the Orléans sales in London after the French Revolution. When he saw the collection in Pall Mall in 1798, the critic William Hazlitt wrote: "I was staggered when I saw the works…. A new sense came upon me, a new heaven and a new earth stood before me."

The building was begun in 1837, by which time the endowment had grown to more than £40,000, to the designs of George Basevi who had taken a three-year Grand Tour absorbing the architectural splendours of every age. After his tragic death, falling through the floor of the belfry at Ely Cathedral, his work was continued by two brilliant successors — C R Cockerell in 1845–48 and E M Barry from 1870–75. The rich marble staircase embellished in gold has triple barrel vaults and a gorgeous dome supported by caryatids.

At the other end of the scale (and the town) is Kettle's Yard, one of the world's most absorbing and enchanting small galleries of art. It is the home of its founder Jim Ede and his wife Helen. Moving to Cambridge in 1956 they converted four cottages into a house to display his collection of early 20th-century art. There are fine works by Ben Nicholson, Henri Gaudier-Brzeska, Barbara Hepworth, Henry Moore and Christopher Wood as well as Brancusi and Miró.

Newly cleaned, the glistening portico of the Fitzwilliam Museum rivals the British Museum in sheer richness and pomp. Here the architect George Basevi moves on from the chaste elegance of the Regency Greek Revival to full Roman Imperial grandeur reflecting the ascendant British Empire.

The University Museum of Zoology, under refurbishment in 2014, contains numerous skeletons and preserved skins of extinct animals including a 70-foot finback whale skeleton. Some of the fish specimens, stored in spirit, were collected by Darwin on the voyage of HMS Beagle in the 1830s. Here are the fruits of university expeditions to Polynesia and the South Pacific and material from James Cook's famous voyages.

The city's collection of industrial heritage exhibits at the Cambridge Museum of Technology is neatly housed in an 1894 pumping station where household waste originally powered the steam engines which pumped waste to a sewage farm just over two miles away. Two Hathorn Davey steam engines survive, one running on steam at weekends.

The Cambridge Science Centre, on Jesus Lane, was opened in 2013 with an exhibition of the electromagnetic spectrum and the principles of sound and hearing.

The Cambridge and County Folk Museum, now the Cambridge Museum, is housed in eight rooms of the former White Horse Inn. In a city which has produced so many great men, its collection celebrates the lives of ordinary people. Recording local customs, beliefs and songs, exhibits include courting tokens made of corn, moles' paws carried to prevent rheumatism, and blue glass balls hung in windows to protect houses from malevolent spells and trap the reflection of any peering witch.

At New Hall is a collection donated largely by leading women artists in Britain. There are now close to 400 works including a 1986 Tracy Emin. Add to these the Museum of Classical Archaeology on the Sidgwick site with a collection of several hundred casts including the Laocoon, the Farnese Hercules, the Barberini Faun and the Charioteer of Delphi. This has an added rarity value as so many museums are disposing of their collections. The Peplos Kore is a cast of a statue of a young woman painted brightly like the original which was set up on the Acropolis in Athens about 530 BC.

The Museum of Archaeology and Anthropology, reopened in 2013 after a major makeover, contains many local antiquities, while the Whipple Museum of the History of Science has a fascinating collection of scientific instruments.

Cambridge happily escaped the onset of heavy industry in the 19th and 20th centuries and has no counterpart to the Morris car works at Cowley in Oxford. More recently, it has seen the growth of new high-tech industries and the creation of "Silicon Fen". Specialities are software and bioscience, involving many start-up companies that have grown from the university.

The Cambridge Science Park is now the largest commercial Research and Devolopment Centre in Europe, owned by Trinity College. The brainchild of Sir John Bardfield, the enterprising college bursar who turned Trinity into the richest of all Oxbridge Colleges by shrewd investments including Felixstowe Docks, it was established on a 140-acre farm the college had owned since the reign of Henry VIII. When the park celebrated its 40th anniversary, it was home to nearly 100 firms employing more than 5,000 people. During Bradfield's tenure as bursar from 1956 to 1992 when retail prices increased 12 times, the college's external revenues rose nearly 80-fold while the value of its shares rose nearly 30 times. When he began, King's was top of the college wealth list.

Pumping Station
19th Century engineers took pride in waterworks' buildings constructing small pumping stations in good materials to ensure durability and distinctive coloured brick work.

By 2006, Trinity's external revenue was £33m while King's had dropped to third place (behind St John's) with £4.1m. More recently, Trinity's snapped up the lease of the Millennium Dome in Greenwich when its fortunes were at its nadir. Now it is one of the top events' venues in London.

The City's churches are also architecturally remarkable. Most prominent is St Mary the Great, the university church north of King's Parade, known as Great St Mary's to distinguish it from Little St Mary's on Trumpington Street. The Cambridge chimes struck by its clock were adopted for Big Ben.

All Saints in Jesus Lane with its powerful steeple was built by G F Bodley in 1869–71 to replace an earlier medieval church that stood opposite the gate of St John. Bodley's initial High Victorian Ruskinian design proved too expensive and he turned towards a plainer Middle-Pointed style. What emerged was warmly welcomed by the *Ecclesiologist*: "We note, with some satisfaction that Mr Bodley has restricted himself to pure English forms.... The time for a reaction from exclusively French or Italian types has at length arrived." Here Late Victorian Architecture began. It is hard to believe now, but in the 1980s, the Diocese of Ely proposed to demolish the nave leaving only the chancel and the tower. The town rallied to the cause, fired by an exhibition on William Morris at the Fitzwilliam Museum which highlighted the importance of Morris's work at All Saints. Despite such support, it took the casting vote of Robert Runcie, Archbishop of Canterbury, to steer the church into the safe hands of the Churches Conservation Trust.

Holy Sepulchre, known as the Round Church, is one of five circular Norman churches surviving in England (Temple Church in London is the most famous). They are associated with the Templars who served as guardians of the Holy Sepulchre in Jerusalem during the early Crusades. After part of the ambulatory collapsed, the Cambridge Camden Society appointed Anthony Salvin to restore the church which he did with Victorian thoroughness. Its distinctive two-stage form, with a conical roof rising from a drum and an outer aisle with a roof like a skirt, makes it an object of great affection. The circular interior sports stout cylindrical columns supporting arches within arches and an upper tier of twin arches supported by delicate columns on Romanesque cushion capitals.

St Bene't's, with its Anglo-Saxon tower (c 1040–70) of three stages, is the oldest church in the city. Its interior is a surprise after the slightly petite impression it gives on the outside. The aisles, dating from the 1850s–70s, are Victorian rebuildings, the north ones by J R Brandon and the south by A W Blomfield.

The main Catholic church, Our Lady and the English Martyrs, has an immensely powerful presence on Hills Road, the dominating landmark on the way to the station. It is another example of the many foundations made by women in Cambridge. As the parapet proclaims, it was paid for by Mrs Lyne-Stephens. Born in Versailles in 1912 as Pauline (or Yolande) Duvernay, she trained at the Paris Opera Ballet and made her London debut at the Drury Lane Theatre in *Sleeping Beauty*. Her captivating

The Church of the Holy Sepulchre known as The Round Church dates back to 1130 AD and is only one of four in use in the country. It is based on a round church in Jerusalem when the crusading knights returned to England. Their influence helped build round churches of that period.

beauty and dancing enchanted audiences but, in 1837, at the height of her fame she retired marrying Stephens Lyne-Stephens, an English banker and MP reputed to be the richest commoner in England.

After his death in 1861 she continued to live in his splendid Jacobethan mansion near Thetford using her personal fortune to build Our Lady and the English Martyrs in 1885–90. Her architects were Dunn & Hanson of Newcastle, a practice which made a specialty of Catholic churches. The tower with its 214-foot spire (65 m) was a forceful gesture in a university which had been a bastion of Anglicans and Protestants since the Reformation.

St Edward King and Martyr, hidden on the north side of the Guildhall in St Edward's Passage, played a key role in the Reformation in England. Here, on Christmas Eve 1525, Robert Barnes, one of a group of evangelicals inspired by Erasmus and Luther, gave a sermon attacking the corruption of the clergy in general and Cardinal Wolsey in particular.

Emmanuel Congregational Church is a prominent landmark in Trumpington Road. Built of Ancaster and York stone, it was designed by Cubitt in 1872–74. By Cambridge standards, it is lacking in refinement, perhaps deliberately so.

While Oxford was blessed with an abundance of fine building stone from nearby quarries, Cambridgeshire has an abundance of clay suitable for brick-making but little stone. King's College Chapel was built initially with Yorkshire limestone supplemented by Weldon stone from Northamptonshire. Ketton stone from Rutland was used increasingly in the 17th century, notably for Wren's Trinity College Library. Wren introduced gleaming white Portland stone from Dorset for his chapel at Pembroke College and it was used for major university buildings in the 19th century but not for colleges. Bricks and tiles were manufactured around Cambridge from the 13th century, while local clays produced many shades of redbrick. White brick, used later for many terrace houses, first appears in Bishop Alcock's work at Jesus just before 1500.

Pembroke Chapel.
This is the first building designed by
Sir Christopher Wren. It was commissioned
by his uncle Matthew Wren, Bishop of
Ely and built in 1663-65. It takes the form
of a classical temple front standing proudly
on Trumpington Street. In place of columns,
there are flat pilasters. Wren chose the
Corinthian Order, richer than Doric or Ionic,
with its acanthus leaf capitals.

The Gatehouse at King's College Cambridge was designed by William Wilkins, the architect of Downing College. Architectural historian, Nikolaus Pevsner, describes it thus: "Wilkins had here designed with gusto. The scale is right, the height is right, the execution is substantial - not mean, like so much neo-Gothic work - and the detail is by no means dull."

Centre of Cambridge

A starting point for any walk through Cambridge is King's Parade. The Senate House is a building so handsome, blemishless and perfect in every detail that it could have stood in Ancient Rome. Across the street is St Mary the Great, the University Church, designed on the pattern of the grandest Perpendicular wool churches with large windows throughout. It is played up cheekily by the Victorian corner tower of Caius (Alfred Waterhouse, of course). A must is to walk down the narrow lane of Senate House Passage beside Caius to admire the exquisite Gate of Honour, an enchantingly youthful example of early Renaissance architecture. Nearby is the Gatehouse of the Old Schools dating from the early 1440s; it is faced with intricate geometric paneling which is one of the glories of the Perpendicular Style.

It is also the perfect prelude to the unrivalled glory of King's College Chapel, thrusting heavenwards with its soaring buttresses and high-set window and pinnacles. The Regency entrance gate and screen to King's Great Court is a telling homage from a classical architect to his medieval predecessor. Beyond is St Catherine's College with its court open to view from the street behind ornamental railings. Across the street is Corpus Christi, sternly intellectual and dating from the 14th century.

North of the Senate House are the attractive shops of Trinity Street including Fitzbillies with its Art Nouveau whiplash curve. Set back is the gatehouse to Trinity, founded by Henry VIII and the largest of the Cambridge colleges. Beyond is the still grander gatehouse of St John's College and beside it the spectacular 1860s Gothic revival Chapel by the great George Gilbert Scott. A hundred yards further on you step back seven centuries to the Norman Round Church of Holy Sepulchre.

The "Festival of Nine Lessons and Carols" is the Christmas Eve service held in King's College Chapel each year. Introduced in 1918, it was first broadcast on the BBC in 1928 and now reaches the homes of millions of people around the world each Christmas.

For over 800 years, students have been receiving their degrees at Cambridge in a ceremony that is conducted in Latin at the Senate House. The neo-classical building in Portland stone acts as the perfect backdrop for this solemn occasion. By custom, candidates from Kings, Trinity and St John's Colleges are presented first, followed by other Colleges in order of foundation by the university.

The Senate House.

St Mary the Great is the University Church. The Nave was begun c. 1488 and the elegant tower was completed in 1593–1608. It dominates the end of King's Parade and faces the beautiful lawn of the Senate House.

Trinity Gateway and St John's

For all the splendour of the college, the buildings respect the curving line of the medieval street. The Tudor gateway is set back to achieve a straight sided court within, leaving the chapel projecting beyond the college court. Beyond is the red brick gatehouse and entrance to St John's College with the powerful tower of the Victorian chapel by Scott behind. The result is that colleges make less of an impact on the street than similar institutions in other countries. Note the two doors in the Trinity gatehouse – a small door on the right for those on foot and a double door for carriages and horses.

College Porters are always smartly dressed and the bowler hat is still worn with great dignity.

St John's Hall, which faces on to First Court, has a fine hammer beam roof, painted in black and gold and decorated with Coats of Arms. Inside, there is handsome panelling which dates from 1528-9, a fine bay screen, surmounted by the Royal Arms, and a hexagonal louvre dating to 1703 above. It is much in demand as a hospitality venue.

St John's Gateway.
The Coat of arms over the entrance to St John's with the red rose of Lancaster and the portcullis flanked by yales – mythical beasts with elephants' tails, antelopes' bodies, goats' heads and spiralling horns.

Commissioned as part of the re-orientation of the entrance to the Divinity School at St John's College, the so called Quincentennial Gate allows for clear views of the distinctive courtyard beyond. The college shield atop the gate bears the arms of the Lady Margaret Beaufort, Countess of Richmond and Derby, mother of Henry VII, after whom the college was founded.

The Wren Library, Neville's Court.

Trinity College, the largest college in Cambridge, was founded by Henry VIII in 1546. The Great Court is the creation of Dr Thomas Nevile, who was appointed master of the college by Elizabeth I in 1593. Completed in 1612, it is larger than any other court in either Cambridge or Oxford. The court's great size disguises its irregularities, and with the Renaissance Fountain in the centre, it is a charming place to wander around and admire the variety of architectural styles.

Nevile was also responsible for Nevile's Court (also 1612), a new court with parallel cloistered ranges to the west of Great Court. Sixty years after construction, the Court was closed in on the west side by Sir Christopher Wren's monumental Library, the architect's masterpiece. Built of Ketton stone, its upper floor houses the single room of the Library itself, while the ground floor was left open "according to the manner of the ancients" as Wren put it.

Interior of the Wren Library.

The Great Court.

Nevile's Court, showing the Hall (1604-05) at centre

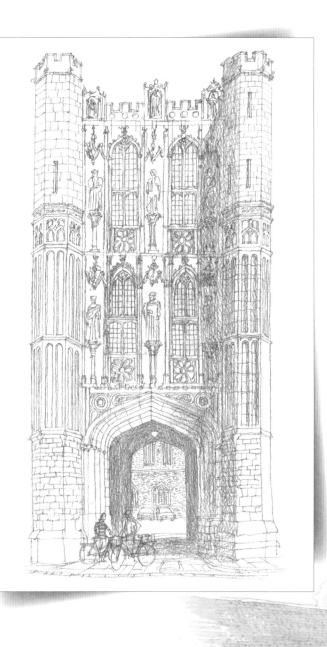

The Old Schools' gate house in Trinity Lane
dates back to 1441-43 and leads through
to West Court which originated with the
first buildings for King's College begun in 1441.

Trinity Hall is between Trinity College
and Clare College. Not to be confused
with Trinity College, its name reflects
that the early colleges were known
as halls. As it was founded in 1350
it is older than Trinity College and
had one of the earliest and largest
enclosed courts including a chapel
in the 14th century.

Clare College, constructed originally in medieval style, is the second oldest college in Cambridge. Its Old Court was rebuilt in the 17th century in a robust Renaissance style, beautifully faced in golden stone with classical detailing and carving and mullion windows. Enclosed on all four sides, it is perfectly formed and open to the sky.

St Catherine's College was founded in 1473 by
a Provost of King's but remained one of the
smallest colleges till the 17th century when
it was laid out as a large three sided
court open to the street as it still
appears today. Main Court was begun
in 1674 in the manner of Sir Christopher
Wren and designed by the mason
Robert Grumbold who worked at Clare
and was Wren's master mason for the
Trinity College Library.

At the end of the Main Court which faces Trumpington
Street there is a fine set of gates with plants and lawn.

Tree Court.

The Gate-Tower.

Gonville & Caius College was founded by two
remarkable commoners — Edmund Gonville
and John Caius — whose combined prowess
illustrates the opportunities open to men
of ability and energy in medieval England.
Caius was responsible for several buildings
rich in Renaissance symbolism, including
three gateways that represent the students'
passage through the college. The grandest,
the Gate of Honour, leads out towards the
Old Schools where the student took his degree
and was built in 1573-75 after Caius's death.

The Gonville and
Caius College gate-tower
has a tall spire, chimney
stacks and a large, very
imposing gateway which
opens on to Trinity Street.
All designed by the Victorian
architect Alfred Waterhouse.

The Pepys Building at Magdalene is
named after the famous diarist whose
papers are lodged here. This is an
enchanting example of Renaissance
detail married to a traditional gabled
front.

Much of Magdalene College gardens are quite charming and border the Cam so can be appreciated by visitors who have hired punts.

Advertising comes in many different ways on bikes and on railings.

Eagle Pub
Opened in 1667 as the Eagle and Child on the north side of Bene't Street, it has a RAF bar at the rear with graffiti of airmen in the second world war on the ceiling and walls. It also served for staff of the Cavendish Laboratory. It was here that Francis Crick announced that he and James Watson had "discovered the secret of life", namely the structure of DNA.

The shopfront of Fitzbillies is one of the most stylish essays in the Art Nouveau style to be found in Britain. Art Nouveau is striking for its expressive curves - here a single arch which sweeps over the door creates a silhouette akin to a giant bun. Note the glazing of the shop door and lettering above.

Situated on St Edward's Passage, G. David Bookseller, fondly known as "Davids", is a Cambridge institution. In 1896, the original G. David, a Parisian bookseller, started selling books from a market stall in Cambridge and, shortly thereafter, moved into the present premises. Today, David's continues to specialise in antiquarian books, fine bindings, second-hand books and publisher's remainders.

Old bike. Very old door.

Portugal Place is a very
pleasant cul-de-sac
with charming terraced
cottages dating back
to the 18th and 19th
century.

PORTUGAL PLACE

Cyclists come in all sorts of different styles on the streets of Cambridge.

Magdalene Street comprises a varied row of houses some of which are examples of pre-Georgian architecture. It leads into Bridge Street and both streets have buildings that are different from its neighbour. Some are jettied (stepped) outwards on each floor in the medieval manner. Pubs and shops make it a popular area for visitors and students.

Magdalene Street

"Hop off and on" tourist bus going down King's Parade.

Bridge Street

Post boxes near the market.

City Rangers attach the small posters on the railings around the city.

Rose Crescent runs from Market Hill to Trinity Street, with an attractive Regency Terrace on one side in white brick and shops below.

Corpus Christi is the only Cambridge College
founded by the generosity of a flourishing
town guild, the Guild of Corpus Christi,
to train pupils in academic learning
and to pray for deceased guild members.

New Court of 1823-27 by William
Wilkins, the architect of Downing
College, is in the Regency Gothic style.

The Corpus Clock of 2008 is set in a doorway
on the outside of the Taylor library at Corpus.
Conceived and funded by John Taylor, it is
a rippling 24 carat gold plated stainless steel
disc displaying the time by opening individual
slits in the clock face. There are three concentric
rings displaying hours, minutes and seconds.

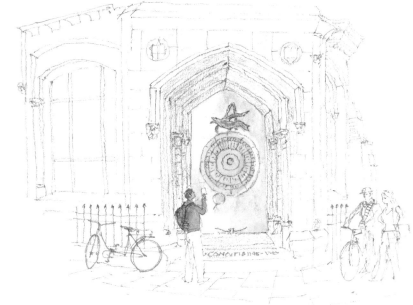

Corpus Christi.
Old Court was completed in 1377 and with
its distinctive buttresses remains the best
and most complete surviving example of a
medieval college court.

BENET STREET

An old bank sign made of stone on
Bene't Street near Corpus Christi's clock.

The Backs

The Backs are one of the legendary sights of Cambridge, renowned for their beauty in all seasons. The expression "the Backs" refers to the backs of the colleges, some standing directly on the water's edge, others with college lawns flowing down to the river. Though the grounds of each college are separate, with their own bridges, paths and gates, they merge into a continuous picturesque composition shaded by lofty trees. This is a perfect example of borrowed landscape by which each set of gardens gains from the view of its neighbours. Starting from the south, the Backs begin with Queens' with its ingenious Mathematical Bridge of 1750. Next is King's with the famous pairing of the Perpendicular Gothic Chapel and the classical Gibbs Building with rooms for both students and dons.

Then comes Clare with its handsome west and south ranges which are among the finest examples of 17th-century architecture in Cambridge, followed by one of the smallest colleges, Trinity Hall. Here the Master's Lodge looks down to the river where the striking 1990s Jerwood Library rises from the water, enlivened by an amazing display of oriel and clerestory windows.

Trinity College beyond is set back from the river with Wren's monumental Library standing by the west gate of New Court which is early 19th-century Tudor Gothic and aligned on the bridge and avenue. Next is St John's with college buildings on both sides of the river linked by the exquisite Bridge of Sighs named after that in Venice but here designed in pretty playful Gothic. This is followed by the Cripps Building, one of the most powerful, indeed overpowering, examples of post-war architecture in Cambridge. Last as the river curves round to the east is Magdalene College with Sir Edwin Lutyens's 1930s Benson Court. On the other side of Magdalene Bridge, punts and boats stand ready for hire.

King's College Chapel, with Clare College on the left and the Gibbs Building on the right.

The architect James Gibbs designed the
monumental Gibbs building (named after
him) at King's, which stands beside King's
Chapel on the Backs. In style and form the
two could hardly be more different and it
is an abiding tribute to Gibbs's genius that
this is one of the best loved and most
photographed groupings in all English
architecture.

St John's New Court looks over the Backs. It was built in 1827–31. Architects were Thomas Rickman & Henry Hutchinson.

The bridge connecting New Court with the College's Third court is the famous Bridge of Sighs (1831) also by Hutchinson.

The delight of the punt on the Cam. Tourists heading upstream from Magdelene Bridge.

King's College Bridge with a line of choristers crossing the Cam on their way from their school to King's Chapel.

The covered bridge, known as the Bridge
of Sighs after that in Venice, is one of
the perennial delights of Cambridge.
It links the medieval courts of St John's
with later courts across the river.

The Mathematical Bridge at Queen's is a
virtuoso display of the carpenters' art neatly
concealing the fact that one end is higher
than the other. The original bridge was
put together with wooden pegs and
was designed by the ingenious William
Etheridge, the foreman on the construction
of London's Westminster Bridge in the 1740s.

The oldest of Cambridge's bridges, Clare Bridge, was built in 1639-40 by Thomas Grumbold in classical style. It is adorned with spherical stone ornaments, one of which has a quarter sphere wedge removed from the back. Every punt operator points this out..... but nobody has an exact explanation as to why this is the case!

The Wren Bridge, built in the style of Wren but not by him, dates around 1709. It is an emphatic display of the mason's art - impressively monumental for what is really just a footbridge.

The Jerwood Library with its prow-like gabled window over looking the Cam is a refreshing combination of modern design and traditional form.

The red brick Elizabethan buildings
of Magdalene College overlook the punts
for hire on the Cam by Magdalene Bridge.
Note the large chimney stacks serving
groups of student rooms clustered
around staircases.

The famous sun dial in Front Court was erected in 1642.

Queens' College is named for two Queens. The first was Margaret of Anjou, wife of the Lancastrian King Henry VI. In 1465 it came under the protection of Elizabeth Woodville, Queen of the Yorkist Edward IV.

Front Court is a complete composition built in 1449-50 to the designs of the king's mason Reginald Ely. The gatehouse has octagonal turrets and a very handsome vault with carved bosses and an original door.

President's Gallery Cloister Court. An impressively large timber framed survival, characterized by close set vertical timber studding and an exceptional degree of symmetry. The bay windows have classical pediments that mark the transition from Gothic to Renaissance forms.

Sidney Sussex College was founded in 1596
under the terms of the will of Frances Sidney,
Countess of Sussex. From Sidney Street, one
sees two courts – Hall Court and Chapel
Court – and the college's third court, Cloister
Court, lies to the north. Chapel Court is
dominated by the stone-faced Chapel,
complete with bell turret and
arched window heads.

The Chapel Court of Sydney Sussex.

Looking East

ambridge began as a market town in the 12th century and rose to hold the greatest annual fair in all England, the Stourbridge Fair. The charm of the market place lies in its informality and it has the rare distinction of hosting a different market every day of the week throughout the year. East of the market, town is more prominent than gown.

Walk down Petty Cury (named for Petit and Cooks) and you come to Christ's, the most modest and ancient of the colleges. South along St Andrew's Street is Emma — short for Emmanuel — and in every sense a beauty stepping from the age of Jane Austen. Across the road is Downing College — ancient Athens brought to Regency Cambridge with its noble Doric and Ionic porticoes. It was also the university's first open campus in contrast to the enclosed courts of older colleges.

Nearby are two of Cambridge's most characteristic open spaces, namely Parker's Piece and Christ's Piece. They are not fenced in like so many town parks and gardens but open greens such as you would find in a country village. Parker's Piece is famous for cricket today and even more as the birthplace of association football.

North of Christ's are two more colleges: First Sidney Sussex secluded behind walls and then Jesus which still retains the medieval priory church of the monastery it replaced. Jesus opens on to Jesus Green and Midsommer Common, both of which border the river Cam. Not surprsisngly, Jesus is renowned above all for its oarsmen (and women now).

Cloister Court, named after the 1890-91 building that faces it, has beautiful gardens. The Cloister itself is characterised by segmental bay windows, shaped gables and a cloister on the west side.

Jesus College Gateway.

Cambridge was less blessed with good building stone than Oxford so many buildings are brick. Though not a 'materiel noble' in the French sense, brick is one of the abiding glories of English architecture with its subtle shades of colour reflecting its rich geology as much as stone. Jesus is approached along a walk enclosed by brick walls. Note the wicket door – a small door set within a larger door to allow those on foot to enter.

Jesus College Cloister Court has yellow-brick four-centred-arched arcades which James Essex in 1762-5 introduced.

Emmanuel College's Front Court contains
Sir Christopher Wren's Chapel and cloister.
Designed in 1666 and completed in 1673,
it has Renaissance motifs.

The Master's lodge at Christ College sports
a charming Coat of Arms dating from
around 1510 above the entrance. Its
wisteria-clad façade in summer faces on
to the First Court.

Christ's College Gatehouse facing
St Andrew's St has a beautifully
carved coat of arms dedicated
to Lady Margaret Beaufort who
was mother of Henry VII. It was
she who helped found the
College in 1506.

One of the Cam's oldest boathouses,
this blue-and-white structure dates
from 1887 and is home to the Boat
Club at Christ's College. Founded in
1830, it was one of only a few
clubs at the time. It has a
notable location, being the only
boathouse upstream (west)
of the Victoria Avenue Bridge.

The Fellows' Building in the Second Court dates from 1640-43 and is one of the most ambitious buildings in the new Classical style, almost like a palazzo.

The Victorian houses on Chesterton Road
over look Jesus Lock and the barges on
the Cam with a view over Jesus Green.

Pembroke Boathouses.
Competitive rowing became a major
university sport in the 19th century
and colleges competed in races to
become head of the river. Several
college boat houses date from this
time, built with overhanging gables
in the manner of Thames-side and
seaside houses. Boats, mainly eights,
were stored on the ground floor with
a club room above.

On the south side of Chesterton Road
there is a cottage terrace with gardens
facing the Cam built in the 19th century.

Sim House is one of the pioneering 'white modern' houses of the 1930s, which form a fascinating chapter in British architecture. Mainly they were a play on cubes, but some architects introduced rounded forms like the two cylinders here. The characteristic metal windows by the Crittal Company remain with predominately horizontal glazing bars.

Willow Walk is an attractive Regency development of a group of streets lined with terrace houses.

The Airport Terminal building (1936) is a rare survival of Pre World War II aviation architecture. A.G.G. Marshall, head of the engineering firm that now uses the terminal as offices, designed it in the International Modern style appropriate to a pioneer industry. The low lines and the all white render are characteristic of the style, as is the bullnose (rounded) projection on the airfield side.

Parker's Piece is one of the group of large flat greens which add to Cambridge's character as an informal garden city. The 25-acre expanse of grass creates memorable vistas. This view shows the University Arms Hotel and the Hobbs Cricket Pavilion, which was built in memory of Sir Jack Hobbs, the great English cricketer, who was born in the city and learned to play cricket here as a boy.

Newnham.
This college still only admits female students.
The Queen Ann Revival Style had a more
domestic feeling than the muscular Gothic
and Tudor found at so many men's colleges.

West of the Cam

For centuries the River Cam formed the boundary for both town and gown on the west of the City. All this changed as the colleges began to build some of the most delightful series of small bridges in all England over the still waters of the Cam. Then, in the later 19th century, new colleges were established across the river, first Newnham, for women, with its lovely domestic architecture, then Selwyn and Ridley Hall in a more masculine Gothic.

The 20th century saw the older colleges expanding beyond the Backs, led by Clare with its lovely Memorial Court. In the 1950s, new college buildings were shoehorned in around old courts but the year 1959 saw Sir Basil Spence's new Erasmus Building on a conspicuous site facing the Backs. With this came a move towards a new monumentality and assertiveness, coined the "New Brutalism". Harvey Court of 1962 by Leslie Martin caused a sensation with its stepped terraces.

Cambridge played a leading and often highly controversial role in the new Modernism of the 1960s and '70s. To the west and north west of the city a series of new colleges was established — Robinson College playing with abstract volumes, Churchill College in its large campus, Murray Edwards (formerly New Hall), Fitzwilliam and Wolfson colleges. The search for building land led the University to expand its teaching facilities along Sidgwick Avenue where the energetic visitor can seek out buildings by leading architects such as Hugh Casson, James Stirling and Norman Foster. Among them stand resplendent late 19th-century and Edwardian villas. Here, too, is the conspicuous tower of the University Library. Further west along Huntingdon Road is Girton College, the University's first college for women, and Michael Hopkins's Schlumberger Centre with a roof as eye-catching as a circus tent.

No less striking is Edward Cullinan's Centre for Mathematical Sciences, with its hint of a distant Tartary, where Stephen Hawking presides. A must for every visitor more to the north is Kettle's Yard, one of the most enchanting small art galleries in Britain.

The college continues the picturesque tradition of Cambridge architecture with its highly varied Dutch-inspired red brick buildings overlooking extensive lawns.

Merton Hall is a timber-framed, jettied house dating around the 16th Century and is attached to the School of Pythagoras which faces the open space of Merton Court and is the oldest house in Cambridgeshire dating back to c. 1200.

Selwyn College
A harmonious design by Demetri Porphyrios, one of Britain's contemporary classicists, with a graceful inset arcade. The arches rest directly on the capitals of the columns in the manner of Brunelleschi's Hospital of the Innocents in Florence creating a sense of lightness. Note the hierarchy of the windows which diminish in size towards the top where the dormers have pediments in the late 17th century manner.

Selwyn Old Court has Victorian buildings designed by Sir Arther Bloomfield in a red brick Tudor style. The Chapel facing the Old Court was completed by 1895, and has the feeling of King's College chapel in its exterior design.

The Centre for Mathematical
Sciences is a splendid essay
in a Romantic Modern style
with ventilation towers giving
a hint of distant Tartary.
Laid out as a campus, it was
built in 1998-2001.

Accordia is a large residential development
of 2002-11. It has shared open spaces, including
a green with a great sense of space. It has terrace
houses and mews like private streets and
lines of vent towers echoing the tall chimneys
of early Cambridge colleges.

The architectural practice of Brewer Smith and Brewer was commissioned to design the Chancellor's Centre for Graduate Study at Wolfson College. Completed in 2004, it features a projecting domed centrepiece. The public rooms may be booked for conferences and the like.

Girton College, established in 1869, was England's first residential college for women. It only achieved full college status in 1948 when women were officially admitted to the University.

Kettle's Yard on Castle Street is an unusual art gallery that was founded by H.S. (Jim) Ede and his wife in 1956-7. A permanent collection of 20th century art is housed in four renovated cottages beneath the ancient church of St Peter.

Robinson College, founded in 1980, was a
gift from Sir David Robinson. The building
is an abstract play of geometric shapes
– rectangular, stepped, angled and sloping,
but all the same colour and texture. The
angularity is heightened by placing the
entrance in the corner.

Fitzwilliam College was founded
in 1869 and originally taught
students in a house near the
Fitzwilliam Museum. It moved
to its present site in the 1960s.
It contains many styles of
modern architecture.

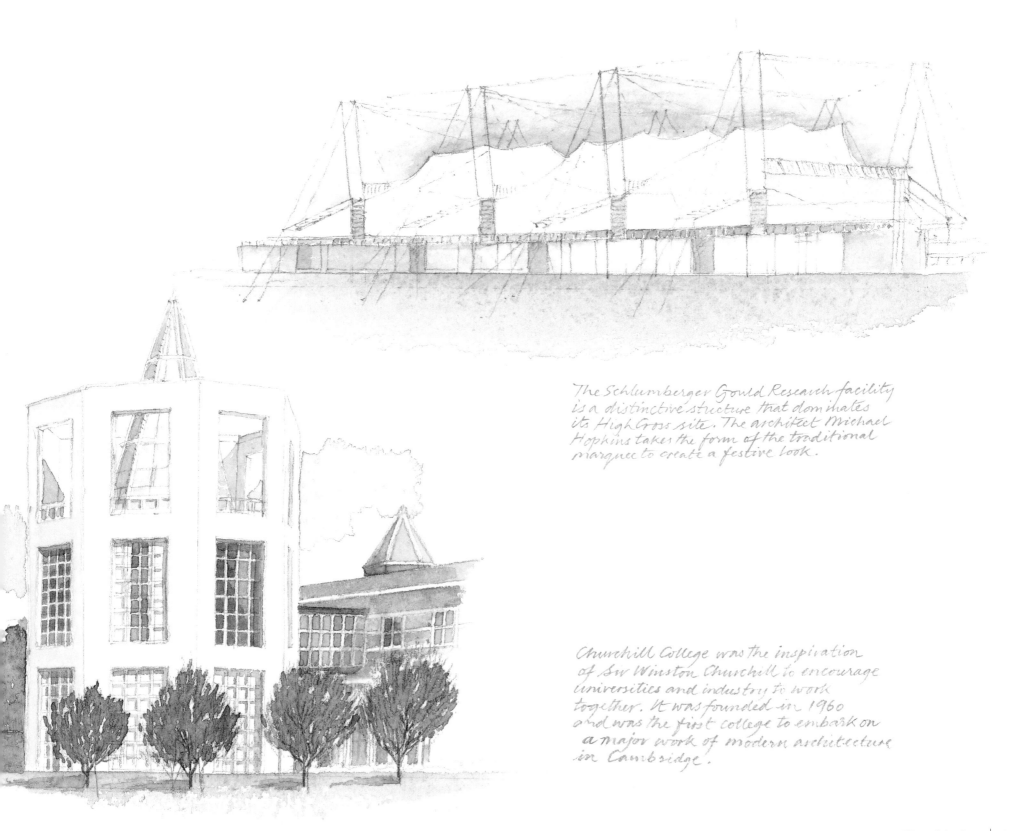

The Schlumberger Gould Research facility is a distinctive structure that dominates its High Cross site. The architect Michael Hopkins takes the form of the traditional marquee to create a festive look.

Churchill College was the inspiration of Sir Winston Churchill to encourage universities and industry to work together. It was founded in 1960 and was the first college to embark on a major work of modern architecture in Cambridge.

South of the Mill Pool

ill Lane and Silver Street take pedestrians, cyclists and traffic across the Cam to Mill Pool where the river opens out into a broad reach and many punts are moored invitingly. They can be manhandled around the weir above Mill Pool by means of rollers.

Here is one of the best Cambridge buildings of the 1990s, Jeremy Dixon and Edward Jones's Study Centre, making brilliant use of a narrow slice of land along the water.

Continuing down Trumpington Street the long front of Pembroke College is nobly accented by Christopher Wren's chapel, designed like a classical temple front. Almost opposite is Peterhouse, founded in 1280, also with its chapel proudly turned to the street, mixing Gothic and Classical motifs.

Immediately beyond is Cambridge's mightiest civic building, the powerful eight column portico and colonnade of the Fitzwilliam Museum (1836–45) revealed in full Imperial splendour after cleaning in 2014. Across the street is Old Addenbrooke's Hospital spectacularly transformed in Post Modern style as the Cambridge Judge Business School by John Outram with an interior in vibrant colours.

Continuing south, and perhaps following the towpath through the meadows, you come to Grantchester, the most attractive of the villages around Cambridge. Here is the delightful parish clock, forever famous from Rupert Brooke's nostalgic 1912 poem "The Old Vicarage, Grantchester", and today the home of novelist Jeffrey Archer and his wife Mary Archer.

The Mill Pool.
From the Mill Pool and its weir, the river can be followed upstream through meadows to the village of Grantchester. By means of rollers, punts can be raised from the lower level along the Backs to the higher water above the weir. In the river are the remains of a submerged tow path. As colleges did not permit barge horses along the Backs, they waded up the Cam to the mill.

The Anchor Pub near Silver Bridge
looking over the Mill Pool. One of
the favourites for students and
punt operators and tourists alike.

To the left is Pembroke Library and the Red
Building beyond that faces Trumpington Street,
both designed in the 1880s by Alfred Waterhouse.
To the right is Wren's Library (1663-5) and behind
Little St Mary's church.

The statue of William Pitt, beside Pembroke College library. Pitt was a student at the college and was 28 when he became Britain's youngest Prime Minister. He is portrayed in the dress of a Roman senator.

Chimneys of Pembroke College on Pembroke Street are strikingly tall and served student rooms. Leaded windows have Tudor hood moulds to throw rain off. Large wooden dormer windows in the roof have steep gables crowned with finials.

Pembroke College on Trumpington Street has the oldest gatehouse lodge in Cambridge.

Pembroke College Court.
Pointed arches to the windows and doors
announce its medieval origin. The four
tall paired windows lighting the hall
are round arched. Much of the college
courts derives from the immaculate
lawns. Both students and visitors must
keep to the sides. Colour is added by
well tended borders creating a domestic
not institutional feel.

Peterhouse College was founded by Hugh de Balsham, Bishop of Ely, in 1280 for scholars "living according to the rule of Merton (Oxford)". After sharing with the secular brethren of St John (forerunners of St John's College) they moved to two hostels by the church of St Peter - from which derives the name of Peterhouse.

Peterhouse Chapel
Architectural styles have often reflected revivals as much as innovation. This chapel curiously mixes Gothic and Classical motifs, reflecting the high church worship it was built to celebrate. Note the paired columns flanking the entrance and the elongated Corinthian pilasters at the angles of the upper floor contrasting with the central pointed arched window.

Little St Mary's church, dating from the early 1300s, served as Peterhouse's chapel. George Washington's uncle was once the vicar and his family coat of arms with an eagle, stars and stripes can be found inside the church. It is said to be the inspiration of the US flag.

During renovation of the Hall at Pembroke College in the 19th century, the doorcase was moved and placed within this wall leading from Ivy Court to the garden. Built in classic style, it bears the College Coat of Arms at its apex.

Fitzwilliam Museum's grandeur continues inside as well as outside. The rich marble staircase is huge and has triple barrel vaults and a gorgeous dome supported by caryatids.

His rather weak design has been spectacularly transformed by another architect, John Outram, in 1991-95. A bold new top storey was added giving the frontage a commanding presence and Wyatt's colour brilliantly played up.

Old Addenbrooke's Hospital is now the Judge Institute of Management. The Victorian Hospital, set well back from the street, was by Matthew Digby Wyatt a leading exponent of Victorian polychromy.

Inside the vibrant colour continues. John Outram's flamboyant and colourful interior is a modern replay of Ancient Egypt with massive columns and a brilliant livery of red, blues and yellows. The drama of the atrium is heightened by the flying staircases that zig zag from side to side.

The Scott Polar Research Institute on Lensfield Road was built by Sir Herbert Baker and A.T. Scott in 1933-4. A delightful building, it has the look of an 18th century pleasure pavilion.

Inside, there is a collection of polar artefacts, journals, paintings, photographs, clothing and maps and the institute is regularly open to visitors.

Sedgwick Museum of Earth Sciences on the Downing site on Downing St houses an important international collection of fossils. It also contains the most intact geological collection in the UK, donated by Dr John Woodward (1665-1728).

The courtyard has an unusual staircase with bear and bison supporters carved by Farmer and Brindley.

The Old Granary of Darwin College
faces the river. It has timber
balconies painted white, a Gothic
style oriel, well proportioned windows
and with the river, punts and trees
makes a delightful scene.

Hobson's Conduit was built in 1610-14 by
Thomas Hobson to bring fresh water to
the city from the springs of Nine Wells
near the village of Great Shelford. Its
route is visible in the broad gutters
running past Peterhouse College
along Trumpington Street.

Quite near the Botanical Gardens on Trumpington Road there is a mile stone. It is believed to be the first ever to be erected in England.

MILE TO GREAT SAINT MARIES CHURCH CAMBRIDGE

Since its opening in 1846, the Cambridge University Botanic Garden has been an inspiration for gardeners and scientists alike. To the north of the garden is a range of glass houses that have been extensively refurbished and reorganised in recent years. As is to be expected there are large-scale collections of tropical plants, as well as cacti, alpine specimens and species from Australia and South Africa.

A beautiful view of the large
Gothic Revival church built
between 1885-90 called Our
Lady and the English Martyrs
Church. A scene from Downing
College looking westwards.

Downing College
In contrast to the usual quads or courts
Downing College has an open campus layout
with long ranges looking over extensive lawns.
It is one of the finest examples of Greek Revival
in England.

The new Downing College library by classical
architect Quinlan Terry has a Greek Doric
portico with fluted baseless columns in
the ancient Greek manner.

Situated south west of Cambridge is the picturesque village of Trumpington, mentioned in the Domesday Book and also in Chaucer's "Reeve's Tale" which is set in the village. Parts of the present church, dedicated to St Mary and St Michael, date from the mid 13th century; it is noted for containing the monumental brass of Sir Roger de Trumpington, a crusader knight (1289). It is thought to be the second oldest brass in England.

A pleasant half hour's stroll brings one to the village of Grantchester easily accessible by punt or by foot from Cambridge itself. A pretty village, with charming pubs and famous tea rooms, it is said to house a high number of Nobel prize winners. Famous former resident, Rupert Brooke, wrote a poem about homesickness set in Grantchester. In it he refers to the church of St Andrew and St Mary on the outskirts of the village: "Stands the Church clock at ten to three? / And is there honey still for tea?".

The church of St Andrew and St Mary.

The Old Vicarage in Grantchester dating from 1683, was the former home of Henry and Florence Neeve from whom, in 1911-13, the poet Rupert Brooke rented a room and later a large part of the house. His nostalgic poem "The Old Vicarage, Grantchester" was written in a Berlin café in 1912. The present owners, the author Jeffrey Archer and his wife the scientist Mary Archer, commissioned the statue of Brooke that stands on the lawn.

Typical of the architecture of the village, a row of 17th century thatched and whitewashed cottages set behind a traditional picket fence.

Also traditional is the tea to be had at The Orchard Tea Garden, operating since 1897. In fact, the orchard, first planted in 1868, came a tea garden purely by chance, when a group of Cambridge students asked their landlady at Orchard House, if they could have their tea beneath the blossoming fruit trees rather than, as was usual, on the front lawn of the house. One hundred and twenty years on, the tradition continues.

College Index

Christ's College was first established as God's House in 1437 by William Bingham, rector of St John Zachary in London, for training grammar school masters. He had petitioned Henry VI, lamenting the closure of no less than 70 grammar schools between Southampton and Ripon in the previous 50 years, and his project had the support of John Brokley, Mayor of London in 1433–4, and other city figures.

The King had other ideas — to expropriate God's House for his new college of King's. Only Bingham's tenacity and energy prevented his foundation vanishing into oblivion and in 1446 he acquired a large alternative site on St Andrew's Street, where, in 1448, he became head of his new college by writ of the king. Three years later he was dead, but his foundation was taken on by Lady Margaret Beaufort, mother of Henry VII, who in 1505 obtained a royal charter to re-found it as Christ's College. (This she did at the prompting of her confessor John Fisher, Bishop of Rochester, who, with funds provided in her will, was the founding force of St John's College).

First Court at Christ's was built quickly following the re-foundation from 1505 to *circa* 1511 with a splendid gatehouse and lavish coat of arms. The master mason was William Swayn, also engaged at St John's, thereby implying that he may have designed both. The court itself was faced in smooth ashlar stone by James Essex in 1758–70. G G Scott Junior reconstructed the 16th-century hall in 1885–79. The Fellows' Building in the Second Court dates from 1640–43 and is one of the most ambitious buildings in the new Classical style, almost like a *palazzo*.

Clare College was founded in 1326 and is Cambridge's second oldest college. Spanning the River Cam, it is set between Old Schools and the University Library. It is named after Elizabeth de Clare, an heiress and the youngest of three daughters of Gilbert de Clare, Earl of Hertford. When her brother was killed at the Battle of Bannockburn in 1314, aged 23, his extensive property was divided between his three sisters. Surviving three husbands, she styled herself the Lady of Clare after her principal estate in Suffolk. Her household accounts shows she lived on a grand scale with a house in London beside the Convent of the Minoresses outside Aldgate, embarking on frequent pilgrimages to Canterbury, Walsingham and Bromholm. (Her largest religious bequests were to Clare and the Minoresses).

The medieval Old Court was rebuilt in the 17th century in a robust Renaissance style, beautifully faced in golden stone with both Classical detailing and carving and mullion windows. The East Range of 1638–40 is by the master builder John Westley with matching west and south ranges by the master mason Robert Grumbold. The external fronts looking out over the Backs have a grace and calm that makes the perfect foil for the majestic silhouette of King's College Chapel. Memorial Court across the river was built between the wars to the designs of Sir Giles Gilbert Scott in memory of the Clare men who had lost their lives.

Corpus Christi is the only Cambridge College founded by the generosity of a flourishing town guild, the Guild of Corpus Christi, to train pupils in academic learning and to pray for deceased guild members. Soon after, it was joined by the Guild of the Blessed Virgin Mary. The royal license was granted in 1352 shortly after the Black Death. Old Court was completed by 1377 and, with its distinctive buttresses, remains the best and most complete surviving example of a medieval college court. New Court of 1823–27 by William Wilkins, the architect of Downing College, is in the Regency Gothic style.

Churchill College, named after Sir Winston, Britain's wartime leader, was approved by the University Senate in 1958. The large 42-acre site was north of the town and the new college for 500 students and 60 Fellows was generously supported by industry and completed in 1967. The architects, Richard Sheppard Robson & Partners, was chosen in a competition that attracted 20 leading practices with rising stars of the younger generation. The Møller Centre, comprising music and conference facilities, was designed by the Danish architect Henning Larsen from 1989–92.

Downing College was founded in 1800 after a prolonged battle over the will of its benefactor Sir George Downing, Baronet, whose grandfather, also Sir George, gave his name to Downing Street in London and was the largest landowner in Cambridgeshire. The college was begun in 1807 to the designs of the young William Wilkins (not yet 30) and is a masterpiece in the Greek Revival style, laid out as a campus rather than a quad. It precedes the famous campus laid out ten years later by Thomas Jefferson at the University of Virginia. Wilkins' long stone ranges have noble six column Greek Ionic porticoes. In 1929 Sir Herbert Baker was commissioned to build a new north range which he characteristically provided with a portico noticeably grander than Wilkins' and diluted the purity of the earlier work by introducing a third storey beneath the eaves. The college has stayed loyal to the Classical tradition first with Quinlan Terry's Greek Doric

Maitland Robinson Library of 1991–94 and then his Howard Building of 1983–86.

Emmanuel College was founded in 1584 by Sir Walter Mildmay and, with Sidney Sussex, is one of two Elizabethan foundations both distinctly Puritan. The site was a former friary.

The handsome low-slung Georgian entrance range was built in 1771–5 by James Essex, architect of many felicitous additions to Cambridge Colleges, who also refitted Emmanuel's Hall. New Court was the original court with the hall on the south. This leads to Front Court with the imposing Brick Building of 1633–34. This was followed by Sir Christopher Wren's chapel and cloister designed in 1666 and completed in 1673 with Renaissance motifs a little more hesitant than at Wren's Chapel at Peterhouse. The lovely Fellows' Garden has extensive lawns and a pond. The Queen's Building of 1993–95, containing a fine auditorium, is by Sir Michael Hopkins and Partners, architects of the pioneering Schlumberger Building.

Fitzwilliam College, founded in 1869, moved to new buildings designed by Sir Denys Lasdun in 1958 to a plan never completed. His are Tree Court and Fellows' Court in purple engineering brick with bands of concrete rather than stone. New Court was built to designs of MacCormac Jamieson Prichard & Wright in 1984–6 in a similar dark brick with a lively system of staircases. They also designed the chapel in 1990–1.

Girton College, established in 1869, was England's first residential college for women, though it only achieved full college status in 1948 when women were officially admitted to the university. It was built to a severe design in a rather dull red brick by Alfred Waterhouse in 1882–87. A tower and spires, numerous gables and soaring chimney enliven the facade which looks best from the extensive lawns to the south.

Gonville & Caius was founded by two remarkable commoners whose prowess illustrates the opportunities open to men of ability and energy in medieval England. Edmund Gonville came from a French family which settled in Norfolk and prospered. A rector of several prosperous livings, he was also a man of business who lent the king money and was rewarded with the title of King's Clerk. He helped found a house of Dominican Friars at Thetford in 1335 and a college for five chantry chaplains at Rushford. Edward III granted him letters patent in 1348 to found the college that took his name.

John Caius, another Norfolk man, came to Gonville in 1529; he was a student of theology in thrall to Erasmus, one of whose books he translated into English. Elected a Fellow, his interests turned to medicine and in 1539 he set out for Padua, the leading medical university in Europe where he shared a house with the brilliant young Vesalius who had been appointed to teach anatomy. Caius gained an interest in the healing methods of the Ancient Greek physician Galen and his texts on botany, zoology and anatomy. Returning to England, Henry VIII asked him in 1546 to deliver a series of anatomical demonstrations at the London Barber-Surgeons that continued for 20 years. He became a very prosperous London physician and, possibly because of his Catholic sympathies, he was granted a royal charter to re-found his college as Gonville

and Caius, transferring to it extensive landed properties. His new buildings at the college were rich in Renaissance symbolism.

Caius' three gateways symbolized the students' passage through the college, with Virtue leading to Honour. The Gate of Humility (1565) survives reconstructed. The Gate of Virtue is dated 1567. The grandest, the Gate of Honour, leads out towards the Old Schools where the student took his degree and was built in 1573–75 after Caius's death. It is traditionally attributed to Theodore Haveus of Cleves, the mason who made Caius's monument. Humfrey Lovell, Master Mason of the Royal Works has also been suggested.

Gonville Court survives from the medieval college. Tree Court is by Alfred Waterhouse in 1868–70 with elements of Loire chateaux architecture with a handsome gate tower, here with the civic grandeur of a northern town hall. St Michael's Court of 1901–3 is by Aston Webb & Ingress Bell, accomplished Edwardian architects. Most recent is the richly wrought Fellows Dining Room in revived Greek style by John Simpson.

Jesus College, like Magdalen in Oxford, is remarkable for the extent of its gardens and grounds, a *rus in urbe*. Just as a decayed medieval hospital was suppressed to make way for Magdalen, so the founder of Jesus obtained royal leave to close a Benedictine nunnery and take over its property. This was Bishop Alcock of Ely one of the most adroit statesmen of the late 15th century who retained the confidence of both Yorkist and Lancastrian kings and in 1485 was made Chancellor of the realm by Henry VII and opened the king's first Parliament with a sermon. The next year he was rewarded with the rich see of Ely. He was Comptroller of the Works to Henry VII and a keen builder himself, founding what became Hull Grammar School and building a new great hall at the Bishop's Palace in Ely where he added the glorious chantry chapel in the cathedral, completed after his death.

The large college is set well back from Jesus Lane and approached along a walled walk known as the Chimney. The battlemented gatehouse opens into First Court and a passage leads through to Cloister Court enlarged from the nuns' cloister and dominated by their church. The yellow brick arcades are the work of James Essex in 1762–65. The chapel is without part of its medieval nave but the north transept is a superb survival of round arched Norman. The 19th century brought major extensions including a large range by Alfred Waterhouse. The new Library of 1994–96 by Eldred Evans & David Shalev is a triumph of contemporary contextual architecture evoking Gothic forms in an abstract manner.

King's College was founded by King Henry VI in 1441 for a rector and 12 scholars from Eton, the school he had founded a year earlier. He took his cue from William of Wykeham who 70 years earlier had founded Winchester College and New College Oxford. His ambitions grew rapidly. In 1453 he provided for 70 fellows and scholars and 16 choristers.

The first stone of the chapel was laid in 1448. It was completed in 1515, towering above the town as Eton College chapel does today. Ambitious plans by Nicholas Hawksmoor (architect of All Souls Oxford) for a new quad were not carried out, but a single splendid block was built to the designs of James Gibbs in 1723–29. It is known as the Gibbs Building. The Great Court was only closed in the 1820s by the gatehouse and screen designed by William

Wilkins, the architect of Downing College. Later additions are by Bodley in the 1890s and Sir Aston Webb after whom Webb's Court is named. In Chetwynd Court Sir G G Scott designed a striking circular staircase.

Magdalene College was founded in 1428 as a hostel for Benedictine monks. The first collegiate buildings were largely paid for by Anne, dowager Duchess of Buckingham. By the time of the Dissolution there was a near complete court with chapel and hall. In 1542 Thomas Lord Audley secured letters patent allowing the college to continue as part of the university. The new name of Magdalene did not reflect Catholic piety but was a play on Audley's name, Magdalene being pronounced like "maudlin". (Magdalen College Oxford is spelt without an e at the end).

The college is most famous for the delightful late 17th-century Pepys Building which houses books left by the great diarist Samuel Pepys. In the early 20th century Magdalene expanded across the street with Benson Court named after A C Benson, the popular author who was master from 1915 to 1925. Sir Edwin Lutyens designed the monumental Benson Court in 1931–32. This was intended to be a three-sided court open to the river and sweeping away the old houses along Magdalene street. Fortunately this did not happen and instead the architect David Roberts converted these and others in a village-like manner as student lodgings.

Newnham College is England's most beautiful example of the 1870s Queen Anne Revival Style, a reaction against the increasing dominance of the Gothic Revival. Characterised by the warm red brick of the Wren period, tall chimneys and large dazzling white

sash windows of varied design, all the college buildings up to 1910 are by Basil Champneys. They are seen to grand advantage along both Sidgwick Avenue and the extensive gardens behind and form a highly varied and inventive group in the best picturesque tradition of Cambridge.

Pembroke College is the third oldest surviving college founded in 1347 for 30 scholars, the year after the Battle of Crecy, by Marie de St Pol, the widow of Aymer de Valence, Earl of Pembroke whose splendid tomb is in Westminster Abbey. The earl was one of the richest and most powerful men of his age with strong connections to the French royal house.

Half of Old Court is of the original 1351–89 build. The rest was faced with smooth cut ashlar stone in 1712–17. The Old Library has a 1690 plaster ceiling. The chapel has a special significance as the first completed work of Sir Christopher Wren built in 1663–5 and begun the same year as Wren's Sheldonian Theatre in Oxford which took longer to complete. It was paid for by Wren's uncle, Matthew, Bishop of Ely, who three decades earlier had founded the chapel at Peterhouse opposite Pembroke. Nineteenth-century additions are by Alfred Waterhouse, including the muscular Red Brick Buildings in a Gothic style inspired by Louis XII in France. Here is a statue of the younger Pitt by Sir Robert Westmacott. Waterhouse also designed the Master's Lodge of 1871–3. The New Court building of 1880–3 is by the younger G G Scott. Orchard Building is by Marshall Sisson in the manner of a Georgian terrace while Foundress Court of 1995–97 is by Eric Parry Architects.

Peterhouse College was founded by Hugh de Balsham, Bishop of Ely, in 1280 for scholars "living according to the rule of Merton [Oxford]". After sharing with the secular brethren of St John (forerunners of St John's College), they moved to two hostels by the church of St Peter — from which derives the name of Peterhouse.

The chapel on Trumpington Street with linking cloisters now makes the east side of the medieval court. The hall remains Cambridge's oldest surviving college building though heightened in the 15th century and much restored by Giles Gilbert Scott Junior. The chapel, consecrated in 1632, is a remarkable example of Gothic motifs mingled with Classical ones, a combination of a deep conservatism engaging with latest fashion. Gisborne Court of 1825–6 was designed by W McIntosh Brooks, a graduate of the college.

Queens' College is named for two Queens. The first was Margaret of Anjou, wife of the Lancastrian King Henry VI. Her foundation emulated his at King's and was for the honour and praise of the *sexe feminine*. In 1465 it came under the protection of Elizabeth Woodville, queen of the Yorkist Edward IV.

The early courts are Front Court and Cloister Court with the tiny Pump Court. Further building followed on the site of a dissolved Carmelite friary acquired in the early 1540s. Front Court is a complete composition built in 1449–50 to designs of the king's mason, Reginald Ely. The gatehouse has octagonal turrets and a very handsome vault with carved bosses and an original door. Cloister Court is reached through the Screens passage of the hall and has cloister arcades and the timber President's Gallery. The river front is notable for its projecting chimneystacks and two-

light windows. The chapel in Walnut Tree Court is by Bodley, built in 1889–91. Friars' Court beyond has Sir Basil Spence's Erasmus Building of 1959–60, the first Modernist arrival on the Backs.

The river is crossed by the Mathematical Bridge where stands Powell & Moya's Cripps Court of 1971–83. Its design continues the theme of their St John's building with dark glass and bronze paneling.

Robinson College was founded by the entrepreneur Sir David Robinson who had made a fortune in television rental and had a large string of winning racehorses. It was built in three years from 1977–80. From the start the college was for men and women. The architects were leading Glasgow Modernists — Gillespie, Kidd & Coia. A competition was held in 1974 for a 12-acre site with mature trees which the architects retained by placing the accommodation in a large citadel-like block with a distinctive corner entrance gatehouse.

St Catharine's College was founded in 1473 by a Provost of King's but remained one of the smallest colleges till the 17th century when it was laid out as a large three-sided court open to the street. The warm red brick gives it a close affinity with civic buildings in London after the Great Fire of 1666. Main Court, begun in 1674, is in the manner of Sir Christopher Wren and was designed by the mason Robert Grumbold who worked at Clare and was Wren's master mason for the Trinity College Library. The accomplished James Essex designed the Ramsden Building completed by 1772. The St Catherine's and King's development by leading Modernist Fellow Atkinson provided accommodation for both colleges and a new dining hall for St Catherine's. Repeated

proposals have been put forward to build a fourth side to the court but these have been resisted leaving the college visible behind imposing gate piers and railings.

St John's College was founded under the will of the mother of Henry VII, Lady Margaret Beaufort in 1511. Six years earlier she had begun Christ's College, encouraged by her confessor John Fisher, Bishop of Rochester who was also to play a key role in the building of St John's. The site was a former Augustinian Hospital. St John's is the second largest college and is rich in the architecture of successive centuries. The turreted Tudor gatehouse has a carved heraldic display picked out in gold. The supporters are yales, mythical beasts with goats' heads, antelopes' bodies and elephants' tails. Above, St John presides in a canopied niche.

First Court was built in 1511–20, with Oliver Scales as clerk of works and William Swayn as master mason, but has been much refaced. The hall with its louvre remains. Second Court was built in 1598–1602, paid for by another munificent lady patron, Mary Countess of Shrewsbury, and designed by Ralph Simons, freemason of Westminster and Gilbert Wigge, freemason of Cambridge.

The smaller Third Court has the Old Library of 1623–25 on its north side. Chapel Court opening from Second Court has a neo-Tudor block dramatically transformed by Edward Cullinan into a new Library in 1992–94. The chapel, built in 1863-69 and powerfully visible from the street outside, is one of George Gilbert Scott's grander creations following on from that he built for Exeter College Oxford. Scott's original design had a slim *flèche*, but in the end a 163-foot imposing tower was built with a donation by the banker Henry Hoare. Scott also designed the imposing red brick Master's Lodge in a rather dour Perpendicular style.

St John's continues on the west of the Cam, approached through the Bridge of Sighs. New Court, across the river, is a match for its commanding position overlooking the Backs. Though it is a symmetrical classical composition, its lively appearance grows from the Perpendicular trim of gables, battlements, turrets and crowning "wedding cake" giving it a lively appearance, enhanced by the pretty cloister range and gatehouse along the front. The architects were the prolific Thomas Rickman and his brilliant pupil Henry Huchinson. Behind, looking over the Cam, is the 1960s Cripps Building: Built to house 191 undergraduates, it is admired as a piece of Cambridge modernism by the leading practice of Powell & Moya. Others were unhappy at its assertive character. It also proved expensive with flaws, notably failed heating systems and leaking roofs.

Selwyn College was founded in 1879, in memory of George Augustus Selwyn, first Bishop of New Zealand, who preached in Maori as soon as he landed. He had competed in the first Oxford and Cambridge boat race at Henley in 1829. The buildings of Old Court are all by Sir Arthur Blomfield, red brick in a Tudor style. The Hall in an Elizabethan style is by Grayson and Ould and dates from 1909. Recent buildings include New Block by Demetri Porphyrios.

Sidney Sussex College was founded in 1595 under the will of Lady Frances Sidney, Dowager Countess of Sussex, on the site of a monastery. The college buildings bear the heavy hand of Sir Jeffrey

Wyatville, who gave Windsor Castle its present grand appearance. In 1822–24 and 1831–33 he remodeled the entire exterior. Under the stucco of Hall Court is the original building of 1595–98 by the Westminster mason Ralph Simons built of three brick ranges with a cross wall to the street. The second court, also with a wall to the street is Chapel Court. Wyatville's best feature is the gatehouse serving ingeniously as an entrance to both courts.

Trinity College was founded by Henry VIII in 1546 incorporating the earlier King's Hall, founded by Edward II in 1317, and Michaelhouse, founded in 1324 by Hervey de Stanton, Edward II's Chancellor of the Exchequer which reverted to the crown on the Dissolution of the Monasteries. The Great Gate was begun *circa* 1490 for King's Hall and the upper stages were not complete till 1535. Trinity Great Court, the largest in the University, is the creation of Dr Thomas Nevile, appointed master of the college by Elizabeth I in 1593.

The sheer size of the Great Court disguises its irregularities — none of the three gateways is centrally placed, and the central Renaissance fountains stand to the side of the main walk across the court to the master's house. The chapel on the north side was begun in the reign of Queen Mary in 1555 and is traditional in design. The long west range includes the Master's Lodge of 1554 and Nevile's Hall of 1604–05 which then also served for theatrical performances. The master mason was Ralph Simons.

Nevile saw Great Court completed in 1612 and immediately embarked on Nevile's Court beyond with cloisters formed of Tuscan columns. The Court was closed in on the west side by

Sir Christopher Wren's monumental Library. The Library on the first floor is 150 feet long running the length of the buildings. The ground floor was left open "according to the manner of the ancients" as Wren put it. To the side New Court was built in 1823–25 by William Wilkins in his familiar Tudor Gothic style. The triple-arched bridge over the Cam of 1763–65 is another work of James Essex.

In the 19th century Trinity expanded across Trinity Street: Whewell's Court was designed by Anthony Salvin in 1859–1868, while lively detail was added at the turn of the century by Caröe. The fierce modern Wolfson Building of 1968–72 was added by the Architects Co-Partnership on a ziggurat plan, followed by Blue Boar Court of 1985–90 planned around traditional staircases with oriel windows and a variety of materials by MJP Architects.

Trinity Hall is tucked away between Trinity College and Clare College without a commanding presence in the town. It was founded in 1350 by William Bateman, Bishop of Norwich, who lost nearly 700 parish priests in the Black Death of the 1340s. Concerned to rebuild the priesthood, his stated aim was "the promotion of divine worship and of canon and civil science [law]". Its name, not to be confused with Trinity College, reflects the fact that the early colleges were known as halls. The chapel was licensed in 1352 and completed in 1366 and 14th-century work survives on the north side of the Front Court and in the North Court. There is a fine Elizabethan library with original benches and bookcases. The Jerwood Library with a prow-like gabled oriel window overlooking the Cam is a masterful and refreshing combination of modern design and traditional form.

Artist's Acknowledgments

It is ten years since the publication of my *Oxford Sketchbook* and I have long wished to complete an "Oxbridge Collection" featuring both universities. So when I was approached by Laurence King Publishers to produce this a book of Cambridge watercolours, I was naturally delighted. The result is this book — *Cambridge: The Watercolour Sketchbook*.

I am enormously grateful of course to my collaborator Marcus Binney, OBE, himself a graduate of Magdalene College, Cambridge who treated me to an exciting journey of the numerous buildings, lanes, courtyards and streets of great beauty which make up the impressive architectural history of this majestic university city. Marcus and I collaborated together on my *London Sketchbook* and I was delighted when he agreed to contribute to this project with his impressive and authoritative narrative.

I am indebted to the work of the Talisman team in Singapore — Norreha Sayuti, Foo Chee Ying, Stephy Chee and Janice Ng — who worked tirelessly to complete the design and layout and also to Kim Inglis, my patient and supportive editor.

As always, thanks are due to my great friend Jayne Norris, who has always had such enthusiasm and knowledge for all my books and for her kind hospitality as ever. In Cambridge, I would like to acknowledge my friend Jo Hawtrey-Woore for her help and support whilst staying in the city.

Finally, I would like to acknowledge the reader who I hope will find my watercolours and Marcus's descriptive writing a fitting tribute to the history of this visually stunning city.

Twice a year the university hosts two sets of "Bumps races" – races where a number of boats chase each other in single file on the Cam, each crew attempting to catch and "bump" the boat in front without being caught by the boat behind. Most colleges enter several crews.

Two college porters in conversation at the gates of Trinity College on The Avenue which faces the river Cam.